Tips & Quotes

Music Stuff I Listen to

My Notes, Lists & Doodles

Compiled by Kitty Edwards

Created by Flame Tree Studio

Publisher and Creative Director: Nick Wells
Senior Project Editor: Catherine Taylor
Art Director and Layout Design: Mike Spender

Special thanks to: Emma Scigliano and Amanda Justice

Created by Flame Tree Studio

FLAME TREE PUBLISHING
6 Melbray Mews
Fulham, London SW6 3NS
United Kingdom

www.flametreepublishing.com

First published 2016

16 18 20 19 17
1 3 5 7 9 10 8 6 4 2

Images courtesy of Shutterstock.com and the following contributors:
alicedaniel, antoninaart, AuraLux, balabolka, dandoo, grmarc, mhatzapa,
mimsmash, Netkoff, Nikolaeva, nmfotograf, Orfeev, Saint A, Tom and Kwikki,
worldion, Natasha Pankina, Pat J M, Yoko Design.

ISBN 978-1-78664-053-6

Printed in China

Contents

Top Tracks

Lyrics/music by:

'Music is nothing separate from me. It is me ... You'd have to remove the music surgically.' Ray Charles

Musicians:

My review (brief):

My review (long):

SONG

'If music be the food of love, play on, / Give me excess of it; that surfeiting, / The appetite may sicken, and so die.' William Shakespeare, "Twelfth Night"

Top Tracks

lyrics / music by:

Musicians:

My review (brief):

My review (long):

music

Top Tracks

Lyrics/ music by:

Musicians:

My review (brief):

My review (long):

'Listen. Can you hear it? The music. I can hear it everywhere. In the wind… in the air… in the light. It's all around us. All you have to do is open yourself up.' August Rush

Top Tracks

Lyrics/ music by:

Musicians:

My review (brief):

My review (long):

Top Tracks

Lyrics/music by:

Musicians:

My review (brief):

My review (long):

MUSIC

Top Tracks

Lyrics/music by:

Musicians:

My review (brief):

My review (long):

"'Ah, music,' he said, wiping his eyes. 'A magic beyond all we do here!'" J.K. Rowling, "Harry Potter and the Sorcerer's Stone"

Top Tracks

Lyrics/ music by:

Musicians:

My review (brief):

My review (long):

'To achieve great things, two things are needed; a plan, and not quite enough time.' Leonard Bernstein

Top Tracks

Lyrics / music by:

Musicians:

My review (brief):

My review (long):

'Music is to the soul what words are to the mind.' Modest Mouse, "Good News for People Who Love Bad News"

Top Tracks for Travel

'Some people have lives; some people have music.' John Green, "Will Grayson, Will Grayson"

' Where words
leave off,
music begins.'
Heinrich Heine

'A painter paints pictures on canvas. We provide the music, and you provide the silence.' Leopold Stokowski

'I've always thought people would find a lot more pleasure in their routines if they burst into song at significant moments.' John Barrowman

Top Tracks for Study

'When we die, we will turn into songs, and we will hear each other and remember each other.'

'Music makes one feel so romantic – at least it always gets on one's nerves – which is the same thing nowadays.' Oscar Wilde

'Without music to decorate it, time is just a bunch of boring production deadlines or dates by which bills must be paid.' Frank Zappa

Top Tracks for Relaxing

MUSIC STUFF I LISTEN TO: TOP TRACKS

'My heart, which is so full to overflowing, has often been solaced and refreshed by music when sick and weary.' Martin Luther

' When I hear music, I fear no danger. I am invulnerable. I see no foe. I am related to the earliest times, and to the latest.' Henry David Thoreau

'Music can be all things to all men. It is like a great dynamic sun in the center of a solar system which sends out its rays and inspiration in every direction...' Leopold Stokowski

Top Tracks for Workouts

'Music acts like a magic key, to which the most tightly closed heart opens.' Maria Augusta von Trapp

'To stop the flow of music would be like the stopping of time itself, incredible and inconceivable.' Aaron Copland

"Music is an agreeable harmony for the honor of God and the permissible delights of the soul.' Johann Sebastian Bach

Top Tracks for Parties

'Music, once admitted to the soul, becomes a sort of spirit, and never dies.' Edward Bulwer-Lytton

LIVE DANCE

'Too bad people can't always be playing music, maybe then there wouldn't be any more wars.' Margot Benary-Isbert, "Rowan Farm"

'Music has power to create a universe or to destroy a civilization.' Katherine Neville, "The Eight"

Top Happy Tracks

Music

'Music gives a soul to the universe, wings to the mind, flight to the imagination and life to everything.' Plato

'Through music we may wander where we will in time, and find friends in every century.' Helen Thompson

'I would teach children music, physics, and philosophy; but most importantly music, for the patterns in music and all the arts are the keys to learning.' Plato

Top Moody Tracks

'Life is for the living. Death is for the dead. Let life be like music. And death a note unsaid.' Langston Hughes, "The Collected Poems"

'If one should desire to know whether a kingdom is well governed, if its morals are good or bad, the quality of its music will furnish the answer.' Confucius

Top Summer Tracks

'There is no feeling, except the extremes of fear and grief, that does not find relief in music.' George Eliot

Top Tracks to Dance to

'Music is the greatest communication in the world. Even if people don't understand the language that you're singing in, they still know good music when they hear it.' Lou Rawls

'Music can be all things to all men. It is like a great dynamic sun in the center of a solar system which sends out its rays [...] in every direction...' Leopold Stokowski

Best Gig Ever!

Date:

Band:

Where:

My review:

♪ live music

'If I belong to a tradition, it is a tradition that makes the masterpiece tell the performer what to do, and not the performer telling the piece what it should be like.' Alfred Brendel

Best Gig Ever!

Date:

Band:

Where:

My review:

Best Gig Ever!

Date:

Band:

Where:

My review:

Best Gig Ever!

Date:

Band:

Where:

My review:

'I believe that a person's taste in music tells you a lot about them. In some cases, it tells you everything you need to know.' Leila Sales, "This Song Will Save Your Life"

Best Gig Ever!

MUSIC

Date:

Band:

Where:

My review:

'Music is what tells us that the human race is greater than we realize.' Napoleon Bonaparte

Best Gig Ever!

Date:

Band:

Where:

My review:

Best Gig Ever!

Date:

Band:

Where:

My review:

'It is a mistake to think that the practice of my art has become easy to me. [...] no one has given so much care to the study of composition as I.' Wolfgang Amadeus Mozart

Best Gig Ever!

Date:

Band:

Where:

My review:

'But credit for the memorable songs and scores must, of course, go to the brilliant composers and musicians who have been associated with me through the years.' Walt Disney

Best Gig Ever!

Date:

Band:

Where:

My review:

'Music may be the activity that prepared our pre-human ancestors for speech communication and [...] to become humans.' Daniel J. Levitin

Best Gig Ever!

Date:

Band:

Where:

My review:

Best Gig Ever!

Date:

Band:

Where:

My review:

'If I had my life to live over again, I would have made a rule to read some poetry and listen to some music at least once every week.' Charles Darwin

Best Gig Ever!

Date:

Band:

Where:

My review:

'... that's what good music does. It speaks to you. It changes you.' Hannah Harrington, Saving June

Hits

Best Gig Ever!

Date:

Band:

Where:

My review:

'I could always have plenty of music.' George Eliot, "The Mill on the Floss"

'I think I should have no other mortal wants,

Best Gig Ever!

Date:

Band:

Where:

My review:

Rock

Volume

Best Gig Ever!

Date:

Band:

Where:

My review:

'The most exciting rhythms seem unexpected and complex, the most beautiful melodies simple and inevitable.' W. H. Auden

Best Gig Ever!

Date:

Band:

Where:

My review:

Best Festival Ever!

Date:

Name of Festival:

Where:

Bands and artists:

My review:

'You can run any of these pictures and they'd be dragging and boring, but the minute you put music behind them, they have life and vitality they don't get any other way.' Walt Disney

Best Festival Ever!

Date:

Name of Festival:

Where:

Bands and artists:

My review:

Best Festival Ever!

Date:

Name of Festival:

Where:

Bands and artists:

My review:

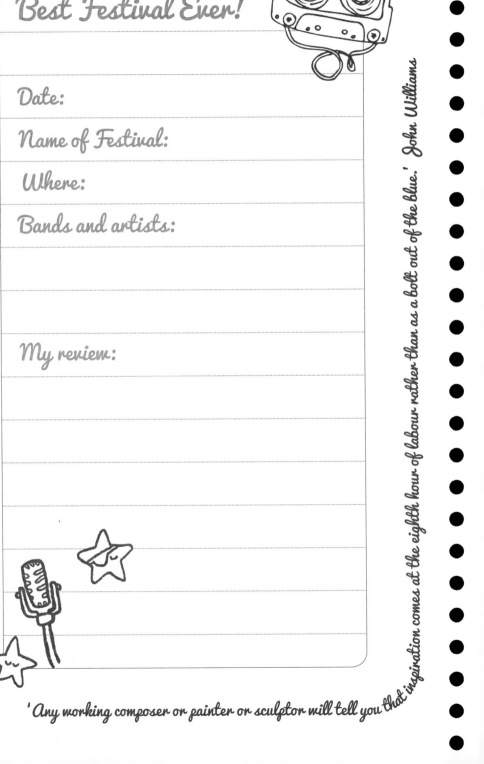

'Any working composer or painter or sculptor will tell you that inspiration comes at the eighth hour of labour rather than as a bolt out of the blue.' John Williams

Best Festival Ever!

Date:

Name of Festival:

Where:

Bands and artists:

My review:

'Pop music provides not just the soundtrack to our lives, as the cliché goes; it releases our emotions and helps us to articulate them.' Sarah Churchwell

MUSIC STUFF I LISTEN TO: GIGS, ALBUMS & VIDEOS

49

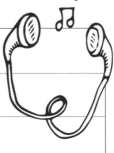

Best Festival Ever!

Date:

Name of Festival:

Where:

Bands and artists:

My review:

'In pop music, the public usually see the results – the hit records, the Grammy Awards performances, the concert tours – but not all the work ...' Bruno Mars

Best Festival Ever!

Date:

Name of Festival:

Where:

Bands and artists:

My review:

'I felt that the elegance of pop music was that it was reflective: we were holding up a mirror to our audience and reflecting them philosophically and spiritually.' Pete Townshend

Top Albums

Title:

Band/artist:

Year released:

My review (brief):

My review (long):

'There are two means of refuge from the misery of life – music and cats.' Albert Schweitzer

'Most people die with their music still locked up inside them.' Benjamin Disraeli

Top Albums

Title:

Band/artist:

Year released:

My review (brief):

My review (long):

Top Albums

Title:

Band/artist:

Year released:

My review (brief):

My review (long):

'Music is the soundtrack to every good and bad time we will ever have.' Alex Gaskarth

Top Albums

Title:

Band/artist:

Year released:

My review (brief):

My review (long):

Top Albums

Title:

Band/artist:

Year released:

My review (brief):

My review (long):

'It's easy to play any musical instrument: all you have to do is touch the right key at the right time and the instrument will play itself.' Johann Sebastian Bach

Top Albums

Title:

Band/artist:

Year released:

My review (brief):

My review (long):

'I tell you such fine music waits in the shadows of hell.' Charles Bukowski, "The Last Night of the Earth Poems"

Top Albums

Title:

Band/artist:

Year released:

My review (brief):

My review (long):

'Musicians don't retire; they stop when there's no more music in them.' Louis Armstrong

Top Albums

Title:

Band/artist:

Year released:

My review (brief):

My review (long):

MUSIC

Top Music Videos

Artist/band:

Song:

My review:

'Music helps us understand where we have come from but, more importantly, what has happened to us.' Simon Van Booy, "Love Begins in Winter: Five Stories"

'Music is nothing else but wild sounds civilized into time and tune.' Thomas Fuller

Top Music Videos

Artist/band:

Song:

My review:

'Oh, the magic of music, with it, all things are possible.' E.A. Bucchianeri, "Brushstrokes of a Gadfly"

Top Music Videos

Artist/band:

Song:

My review:

'Hey Jude, don't make it bad, take a sad song and make it better.' The Beatles, "Hey Jude"

Top Music Videos

Artist/band:

Song:

My review:

Top Music Videos

Artist/band:

Song:

My review:

'As a youngster, I never dreamed there could be a career actually earning a living writing music.' John Williams

Top Music Videos

Artist/band:

Song:

My review:

'So much of what we do is ephemeral and quickly forgotten, even by ourselves, so it's gratifying to have something you have done linger in people's memories.' John Williams

Top Music Videos

Artist/band:

Song:

My review:

'I can't understand why people are frightened of new ideas. I'm frightened of the old ones.' John Cage

Top Music Videos

Artist/band:

Song:

My review:

Heroes

Name:

Band/vocation:

Skills:

Comments:

'Anything can become a musical sound. The wind on telegraph wires is a great sound; get it into your machine and play it and it becomes interesting.' Hans Zimmer

Heroes

Name:

Band/vocation:

Skills:

Comments:

'If something happened where I couldn't write music anymore, it would kill me. It's not just a job. It's not just a hobby. It's why I get up in the morning.' Hans Zimmer

Heroes

Name:

Band/vocation:

Skills:

Comments:

'Tones sound, and roar and storm about me until I have set them down in notes.' Ludwig van Beethoven

Heroes

Name:

Band/vocation:

Skills:

Comments:

Top Artists

Name:

Genre:

Best track:

Band or solo:

Years active:

Comments:

'I like beautiful
melodies telling
me terrible things.'
Tom Waits

'What I like about pop music, and why I'm still attracted to it, is that in the end it becomes our folk music.' Bono

Top Artists

Name:

Genre:

Best track:

Band or solo:

Years active:

Comments:

'But I believe in music the way that some people believe in fairy tales.' August Rush, "August Rush"

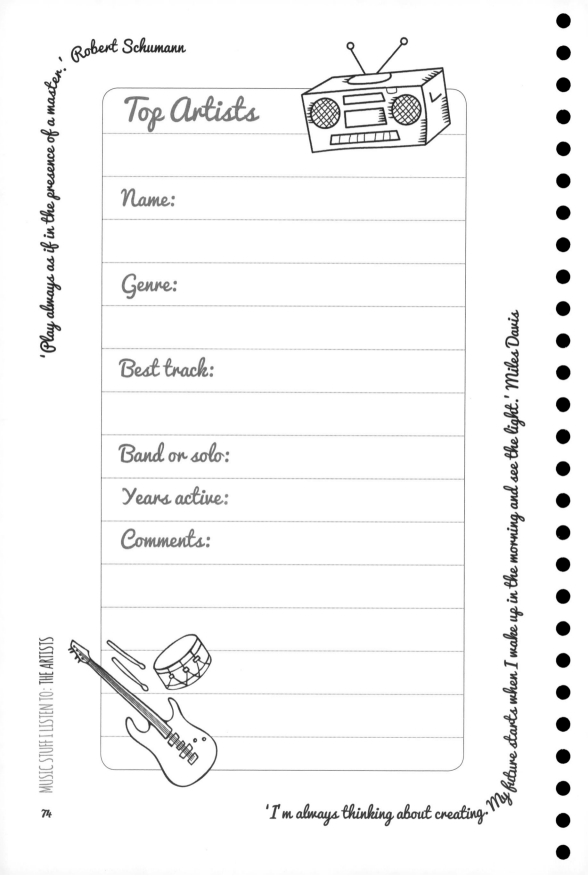

Top Artists

Name:

Genre:

Best track:

Band or solo:

Years active:

Comments:

'My future starts when I wake up in the morning and see the light.' Miles Davis

'I'm always thinking about creating.

Top Artists

Name:

Genre:

Best track:

Band or solo:

Years active:

Comments:

'What do you want to be in the world? I mean the whole world. What do you want to be? Close your eyes and think about that.' Wizard, "August Rush"

Top Artists

Name:

Genre:

Best track:

Band or solo:

Years active:

Comments:

Top Artists

Name:

Genre:

Best track:

Band or solo:

Years active:

Comments:

Top Artists

Name:

Genre:

Best track:

Band or solo:

Years active:

Comments:

'To me, rock music was never meant to be safe. I think there needs to be an element of intrigue, mystery, subversiveness. Your parents should hate it.' Trent Reznor

Top Artists

Name:

Genre:

Best track:

Band or solo:

Years active:

Comments:

MUSIC doodle

Top Bands

Name:

Members:

Genre:

Best track:

Years active:

Comments:

'Life is a lot like jazz - it's best when you improvise.' George Gershwin

Top Bands

Name:

Members:

Genre:

Best track:

Years active:

Comments:

'Music and imagination are made of the same substance - they contain soulful substances that are more real than reality.' Aniekee Tochukwu

Top Bands

Name:

Members:

Genre:

Best track:

Years active:

Comments:

Top Bands

Name:

Members:

Genre:

Best track:

Years active:

Comments:

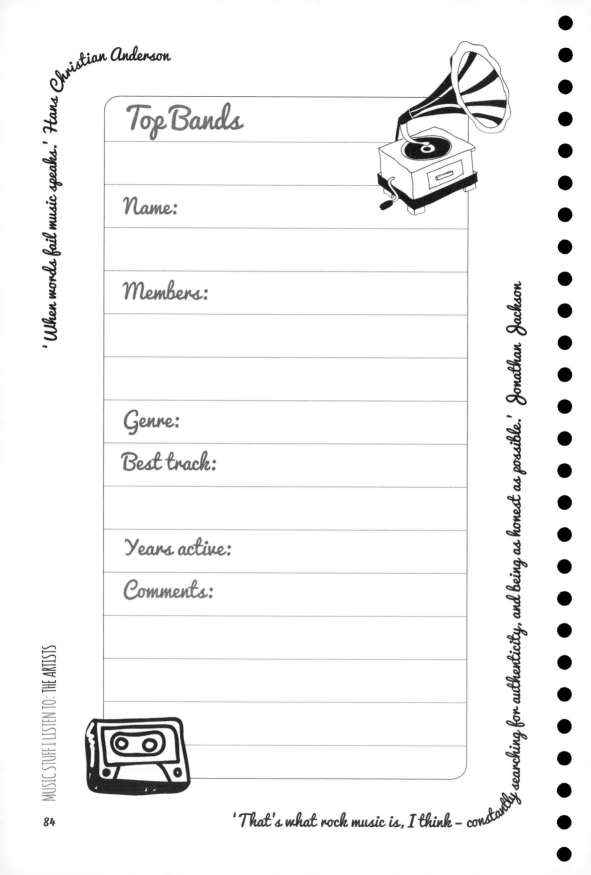

'When words fail music speaks.' Hans Christian Anderson

Top Bands

Name:

Members:

Genre:

Best track:

Years active:

Comments:

'...constantly searching for authenticity, and being as honest as possible.' Jonathan Jackson

'That's what rock music is, I think – constantly

Top Bands

Name:

Members:

Genre:

Best track:

Years active:

Comments:

'For me there is something primitively soothing about this music, and it went straight to my nervous system, making me feel ten feet tall.' Eric Clapton

Top Bands

Name:

Members:

Genre:

Best track:

Years active:

Comments:

'Music is the strongest form of magic.' Marilyn Manson.

Top Bands

Name:

Members:

Genre:

Best track:

Years active:

Comments:

Top Bands

Name:

Members:

Genre:

Best track:

Years active:

Comments:

'Music begins and ends in the air it's got to be shared.' Errollyn Wallen

Top Bands

Name:

Members:

Genre:

Best track:

Years active:

Comments:

Top Bands

Discography #

Name:

Members:

Genre:

Best track:

Years active:

Comments:

A - A - A - d

Top Bands

Name:

Members:

Genre:

Best track:

Years active:

Comments:

FM

Top Bands

Name:

Members:

Genre:

Best track:

Years active:

Comments:

((‹SOUND›))

'You never quit on your music. [...] Cuz anytime something bad happens to you, that's the one place you can escape to and just let it go.' Louis Connelly, "August Rush"

Top Bands

Name:

Members:

Genre:

Best track:

Years active:

Comments:

'He knows the song too? I've never heard this song before! What the hell is it?' Robert, "Enchanted"

Top Bands

Name:

Members:

Genre:

Best track:

Years active:

Comments:

'Without music, life would be a blank to me.'
Jane Austen, "Emma"

'It is the complexity of melody which makes music beautiful, just as negative spaces make a painting work.' Mary Kilbreath

Top Bands

Name:

Members:

Genre:

Best track:

Years active:

Comments:

'... music and thinking are so much alike. In fact you could say music is another way of thinking, or maybe thinking is another kind of music.' Ursula K. LeGuin

To Check Out

List here any new artists or bands you've heard about, to listen to later.

'The woods would be very silent if the only birds that sang were those who sang best...' Henry David Thoreau

'Music is the

fragrance of

the universe.'

Giuseppe Mazzini

'I'm not too articulate when it comes to explaining how I feel about things. But my music does it for me, it really does.' David Bowie

My Song Ideas

Theme:

Key words:

Key notes and riffs:

'Music is worthless unless it can make a complete stranger break down and cry.' Frou Frou "The Dumbing Down of love"

My Song Ideas

Theme:

Key words:

Key notes and riffs:

music

'I think music in itself is healing. It's an explosive expression of humanity. It's something we are all touched by. No matter what culture we're from, everyone loves music.' Billy Joel

My Song Ideas

Theme:

Key words:

Key notes and riffs:

'Music washes away from the soul the dust of everyday life.' Red Auerbach

My Song Ideas

Theme:

Key words:

Key notes and riffs:

'Music is enough for a lifetime, but a lifetime is not enough for music.' Sergei Rachmaninov

Inspiring Songwriters

List here artists and musicians who inspire you with their skill for crafting amazing songs and lyrics.

'He who writes and composes without feeling spoils both his words and his music.' Guillaume de Machaut

'Music must never offend the ear, but must please the listener, or, in other words, must never cease to be music.' Mozart

Inspiring Songwriters

'This will be our reply to violence: to make music more intensely, more beautifully, more devotedly, than ever before.' Leonard Bernstein

'Music is the one incorporeal entrance into the higher world of knowledge which comprehends mankind but which mankind cannot comprehend.' Beethoven

Inspiring Songwriters

'There, in the chords and melodies, is everything I want to say.

'I find myself scribbling on little notepads and pieces of loose paper...' Kurt Cobain

'I've never been a very prolific person, so when creativity flows, it flows.

'Music is your own experience, your own thoughts, your wisdom. If you don't live it, it won't come out of your horn.' Charlie Parker

'It is cruel, you know, that music should be so beautiful. It has the beauty of loneliness and of pain: of strength and freedom.' Benjamin Britten

MUSIC

Inspiring Songwriters

'Thank you for the music / For giving it to me' ABBA

'What would life be? / Without a song or a dance what are we? / So I say

'For in its isolation music has formed itself an organ capable of the most immeasurable expression – the orchestra.' Wilhelm Richard Wagner

Inspiring Songwriters

'Lawrence! Glad to see you're finally getting into the music. Do you get my joke? Because your head is. It's in the tuba.' Prince Naveen, "The Princess and the Frog"

My Songs

'Music is the poetry of the air.' Jean Paul Richter

'Music is the art which is most nigh to tears and memory.' Oscar Wilde

'Without music, life is a journey through a desert.' Pat Conroy

'If you sound great in the practice room, you're practicing the wrong thing.' Berthold Auerbach

My Songs

Wow

'As long as there is a song in your heart, there will always be hopes and dreams.' Patrick N. Nagovan

'Simplicity is the final achievement. After one has played a vast quantity of notes and more notes, it is simplicity that emerges as the crowning reward of art.' Frederic Chopin

POP

'Rock and roll ain't noise pollution.' AC/DC

My Songs

DISCO

Hip Hop

'That's what music is: entertainment. The more you put yourself into it, the more of you comes out in it.' Kurt Cobain

' Jazz will endure as long as people hear it through their feet instead of their brains.' John Philip Sousa

My Songs

'I've always wanted to smash a guitar over someone's head. You just can't do that with a piano.' Elton John

'The musician who always plays on the same string is laughed at.' Horace

'Just remember, music isn't just orchestras and pop stars [...] it's you. Because the music of the spheres is all around you.' Doctor Who, "Music of the Spheres"

Music Calendar

Note here gigs, shows and musical events that you want to attend or watch.

January:

February:

'If I cannot fly, let me sing.' Stephen Sondheim

March:

April:

MP3

'Music is the hardest kind of art. [...] It's hours and hours being put into a work of art that may only last, in reality, for a few moments...but [...] it lasts in our hearts forever.' Daniel Romano

May:

June:

July:

August:

'Truly there would be reason to go mad were it not for music.' Pyotr Ilyich Tchaikovsky

September:

October:

'Music is moonlight in the gloomy night of life.' Jean Paul Richter

Epiphone Guitar Co

November:

December:

'Music expresses feeling and thought, without language; it was below and before speech, and it is above and beyond all words.' Robert G. Ingersoll

Notes & Clippings

Use these pages to note down any other musical musings, lists, memories, doodles or stick/clip in ticket stubs, articles and memorabilia.

'Music is the inarticulate speech of the heart, which cannot be compressed into words, because it is infinite.' Richard Wagner

Clippings

"Music is the art... which most completely realizes the artistic idea and is the condition to which all the other arts are constantly aspiring.' Oscar Wilde

Notes

I ♥ MUSIC ♪

GUITAR

'The chief trouble with jazz is that there is not enough of it...' Don Herold

Clippings

'For me, music and life are all about style.' Miles Davis

'Bands today have to learn their craft by putting the hard work in that we did when we were young performers.' Elton John

Music IS IN the AIR

'A record deal doesn't make you an artist; you make yourself an artist.' Lady Gaga

Notes

'It's when someone sings about their life and what they know, from an authentic place.' Taylor Swift

'My definition of country music is really pretty simple. It's when someone sings about their life and what they know, from an authentic place.' Taylor Swift

Clippings

'Country music is the people's music. It just speaks about real life and about truth and it tells things how they really are.' Faith Hill

Notes

'We paint our own future.' A.P. Sweet, "Dead, but Dreaming"

'We make our own music.

'I only write music for myself. I don't try and appeal to anyone else.' Bryan Adams

Clippings

'To do something that you feel in your heart that's great, you need to make a lot of mistakes. Anything that's successful is a series of mistakes.' Green Day

Notes

'As far as I'm concerned, the essentials of jazz are: melodic improvisation, melodic invention, swing, and instrumental personality.' Mose Allison

'Man, all music is folk music. You ain't never heard no horse sing a song, have you?' Louis Armstrong

Clippings

'I just try to do as good job with the material as I can and play some jazz as well, some improvised music, and do that every night. Just see where it goes.' Mose Allison

Notes

'A verbal art like poetry is reflective; it stops to think. Music is immediate; it goes on to become.' W. H. Auden

Clippings

'You must pass your days in song. Let your whole life be a song.' Sri Sathya Sai Baba

Notes

#MP3

Clippings

'I've never believed in cheapening music by going according to what some people think is public taste.' Les Baxter

Notes

Clippings

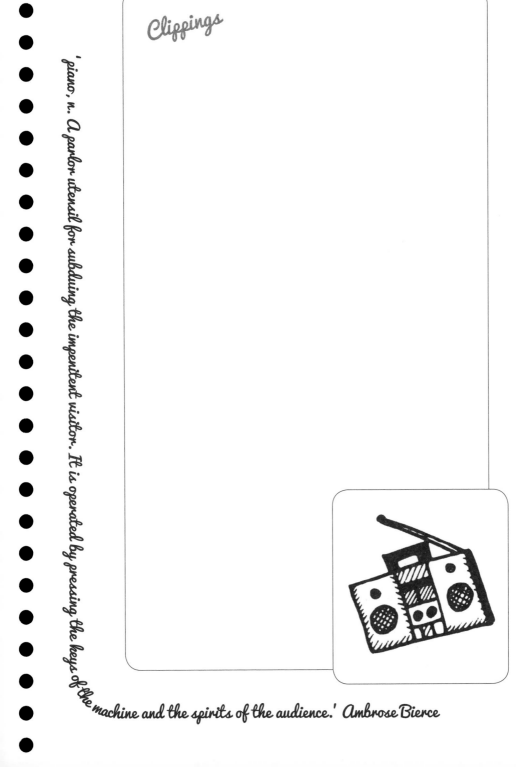

'piano, n. A parlor utensil for subduing the impenitent visitor. It is operated by pressing the keys of the machine and the spirits of the audience.' Ambrose Bierce

ROCK

Notes

'There is perhaps nothing that is not musical. Perhaps there's no moment in life that's not musical... All instruments, musical or not, become instruments.' George Brecht

Clippings

DANCE

'On the other hand, what I like my music to do to me is another the ghosts inside of me. Not the lemons, you understand, but the ghosts.' David Bowie

Notes

MUSIC

DISCO

'Music is edifying, for from time to time it sets the soul in operation.' John Cage

'If you look deep enough you will see music; the heart of nature being everywhere music.' Thomas Carlyle

Clippings

BEAT

Notes

' Jazz is the only music in which the same note can be played night after night but differently each time.' Ornette Coleman

Clippings

'My music had roots which I'd dug up from my own childhood, musical roots buried in the darkest soil.' Ray Charles

Dj
Hip Hop

Notes

♪ Mix Tape ♪
Mix Tape
MIX TAPE ⚡

'The heart of the melody can never be put down on paper.' Pablo Casals

Clippings

'Music is the arithmetic of sounds as optics is the geometry of light.' Claude Debussy

Notes

'A melody is not merely something you can hum.' Aaron Copland

Clippings

' What passion cannot Music raise and quell?' *John Dryden*

'Music is the most abstract of the arts and it expresses the sound of the universe itself.' These are the real rhythms that stimulate the artist's mind and guide his hand.' Robert Genn

Notes

'A song is like a saddle: you ride it for a while, and if it's the right kind of song you can sing it for the rest of your life.' Glen Hansard

Clippings

Notes

RADIO

'If you want to know whether you have written anything worth preserving, sing it to yourself without any accompaniment.' Joseph Haydn

'Only love and music are forever.' Erik. "Phantom of the Opera." (1989)

Clippings

'Words make you think a thought. Music makes you feel a feeling. A song makes you feel a thought.' E.Y. Harburg

Notes

'When people hear good music, it makes them homesick for something they never had, and never will have.' Edgar Watson Home

Clippings

MUSIC

Notes

'In music

the passions

enjoy themselves.'

Friedrich Nietzsche

SOUL

'Never compose anything, unless the not composing of it becomes a positive nuisance to you.' Gustav Holst

Clippings

JAZZ

'For whatever reason, not all people are born with the particular gift of being able to express ourselves through music. And, believe me, it is a gift.' Billy Joel

BLUES

Notes

METAL

'Music is a discipline, and a mistress of order and good manners, she makes the people milder and gentler, more moral and more reasonable.' Martin Luther

Clippings

INDIE

'Heard melodies are sweet, but those unheard / Are sweeter; therefore, ye soft pipes, play on.' John Keats

'Music is the pleasure the human soul experiences from counting without being aware that it is counting.' Gottfried Wilhelm Leibniz

Notes

ROCK

POP

'Music is a bird's answer to the noise and heaviness of words. It puts the mind in a state of exhilarated speechlessness.' Yann Martel

Clippings

'But however measurable, there is much more life in music than mathematics or logic ever dreamed of.' Gabriel Marcel

RaP

MUSIC

Notes

PLAY

'If there had not been music in my life, I would have been a very poor man.' Henri Leopold Masson

'Of all noises, music is the least disagreeable.' Samuel Johnson

Clippings

'But I think a song that is really emotionally packed, with a great melody that just will soar, that's the keeper.' Reba McEntire

Notes

'Music is the surest way of reaching someone else's heart.' Dudley Moore

Clippings

'These seem to me so ambiguous, so vague, so easily misunderstood in comparison to genuine music, which fills the soul with a thousand things better than words.' Felix Mendelssohn

Notes

Clippings

'Music is art in real time. As soon as the brain conceives of a variation it is rendered. It is like painting in public, but much more compressed.' Ben Novak

LOVE

SONG

Notes

SONGS

'People are dying for everything else, so why not the music?' Lou Reed

'The music is all. People should die for it.

Clippings

'If the king loves music, there is little wrong in the land.' Mencius

'Music is the greatest communication in the world. Even if people don't understand the language that you're singing in, they still know good music when they hear it.' Lou Rawls

Notes

'I always thought the band should be called The Whom.' Scott Roeben

'I'm a little obsessive about grammar.'

'Music, when healthy, is the teacher of perfect order, and when depraved, the teacher of perfect disorder.' John Ruskin

Clippings

'This will be our reply to violence: to make music more devotedly, more passionately, more beautifully than ever before.' Leonard Bernstein

Notes

RAP

'The best music is essentially there to provide you something to face the world with.' Bruce Springsteen

Clippings

META

"Music occupies a certain part of the brain, and allows the other senses to float through colour choices, line and design with spontaneity.' Elfrida Schragen

For further journals, notebooks, calendars
and illustrated books on a wide range of subjects,
in various formats, please look at our website:

www.flametreepublishing.com